DON'T BE A PUPPET ON A STRING

Don't be a puppet on a string

BOB & MARILYN DONAHUE

Tyndale House Publishers, Inc., Wheaton, Illinois

Unless otherwise noted, all Scripture references are taken from the *Revised Standard Version* of the Bible.

First printing, June 1983
Library of Congress Catalog Card Number 83-70045
ISBN 0-8423-0610-2
Copyright ©1983 by Bob and Marilyn Donahue
All rights reserved
Printed in the United States of America

CONTENTS

INTRODUCTION
WHO PULLS YOUR STRINGS? 7

ONE
DON'T BLAME ME! 13

TWO
JOIN THE CLUB 23

THREE
PROMISES...PROMISES 33

FOUR
A REAL HIGH 39

FIVE
SEEING STARS: HOROSCOPES, CRYSTAL BALLS,
AND OTHER FORTUNE COOKIES 47

SIX
AND NOW, A WORD FROM
OUR SPONSORS... 53

SEVEN
MANNERS THAT MATTER 59

EIGHT
WHO'S THE MASTER OF YOUR FATE? 67

NINE
QUESTS, QUESTIONS, AND QUANDARIES 75

TEN
STAND UP AND BE COUNTED 81

CONCLUSION
PUT YOUR BEST FOOT FORWARD 87

INTRODUCTION
WHO PULLS YOUR STRINGS?

Puppets have been around for a long time. Historians don't know for sure where they began, but they do know that there were puppets in ancient India, China, and Egypt. Today, puppets are still popular. Puppetry is considered a "theater form." This means that it is used as entertainment—it is a performing art.

There are many different kinds of puppets.

1. **Hand puppets** are the simplest. Sometimes they are called **glove puppets** because they are worn on the puppeteer's hand like a glove. They are also called **finger puppets** because they are small enough to fit on a finger.

2. **Marionettes** are puppets that have strings or wires attached to all their movable parts. It's wonderful to watch them when they are operated by a skilled puppeteer.

3. **Rod puppets** are operated with long, stiff rods, or sticks, instead of strings. One main rod is attached to the head, and other rods manipulate the arms and legs.

4. **Shadow puppets** are also operated with rods, but they are very special because they are brightly painted cutouts that are placed behind a white screen and in front of a light so that the audience sees only the shadows on the screen.

5. **Combination puppets** use any and all methods the puppeteer needs. By combining rods and strings

and gloves, he can achieve unusual and creative effects in his performance.

Puppets can be made from almost any materials available—clay, bone, ivory, wood, wax, cloth, rope, straw, papier-mâché, potatoes, cardboard, plastic, and anything else the puppeteer's imagination can suggest. Anything, that is, except flesh and blood.

This is the catch—no matter how animated a puppet character seems to be, it is not alive. An inanimate object, it only **seems** to have a life of its own. It is the puppeteer who makes it walk and talk and laugh and cry and dance and sing. That's because the puppeteer is in control. The puppeteer decides the WHO, WHAT, WHERE, WHEN, and even the WHY of the puppet's life.

A puppet cannot nod its head or lie down on its back without help from the puppeteer. A puppet cannot talk, for it has no voice of its own. Most important of all, a puppet cannot think because puppets don't have brains.

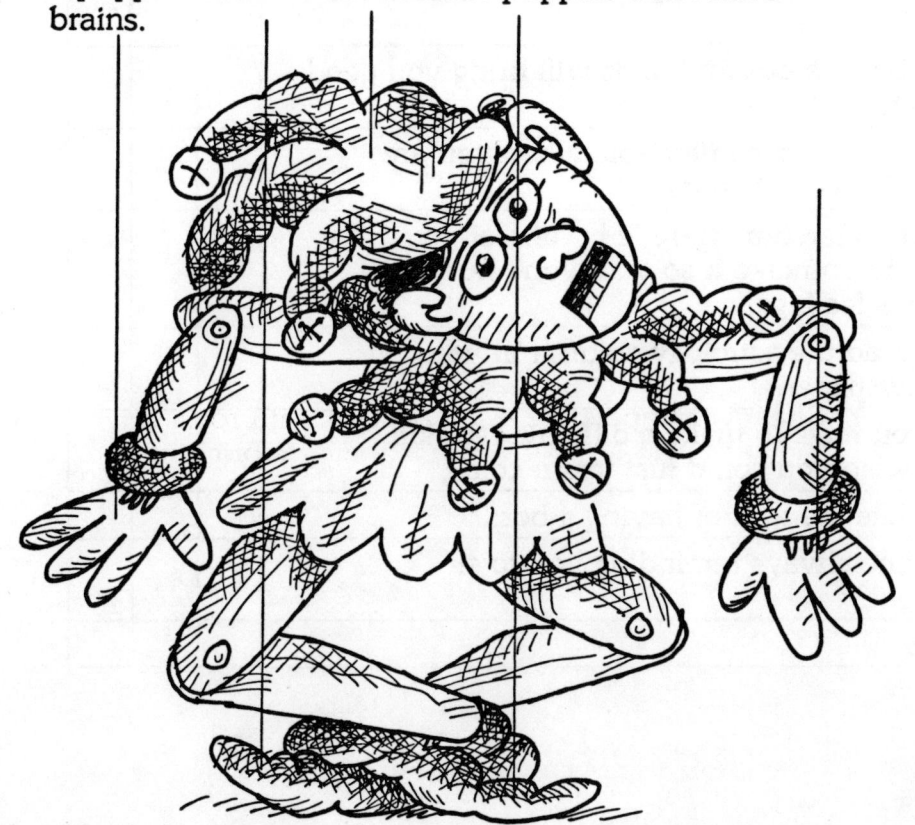

Sometimes people act as if they are puppets. They wait for someone else to pull their strings and make all their decisions for them. Do you know anyone like that? Have you ever acted like a puppet yourself?

Take this **Punch and Judy Quiz** and see if you are a dangler or a doer.

PUNCH AND JUDY QUIZ

	YES	NO	SOMETIMES
1. Do your parents tell you what they want you to do with your future?			
2. Will you do almost anything to be asked to join a special club at school?			
3. When you are asked for your opinion, do you wait and see what other people think before you answer?			
4. Do you believe certain things will bring you good or bad luck?			
5. Do you feel more comfortable when you are dressed like your friends?			
6. If you are offered a cigarette by one of your friends, do you take it so you won't hurt anybody's feelings?			
7. Do you read the astrology column in your daily newspaper?			
8. When you have to make a difficult decision, do you wish you could just toss a coin?			
9. Do you like the idea of having a boss?			
10. Is someone always reminding you to sit up straight?			
TOTALS			

Score your quiz this way:
Yes—**10 points**
No—**0 points**
Sometimes—**5 points**

Now add up ALL your points from all three columns. Your total score is _____.

If you got between 0 and 30, you seem to be a doer instead of a dangler. You are learning to think for yourself, and are on your way to becoming an independent person.

If your score was between 35 and 60, you have the potential to be a doer, but you're going to have to climb down from the "sometimes" fence and learn to make your own decisions.

If your score was between 65 and 85, watch out! You may be dancing to somebody else's tune.

If your score was between 90 and 100, you are in danger of dangling. This means you are letting yourself be manipulated—just like the puppet in the picture.

Everyone feels like dangling sometimes. When the going gets tough, it seems easier to go along with the crowd and let another person make your decisions for you.

But this kind of thinking can be dangerous. It can get you into a lot of trouble. It can also damage your self-respect. Puppets are fascinating to look at. Although they're a lot of fun to watch, nobody really wants to be one, for puppets just hang around, waiting for someone else to pull their strings.

Has anybody been pulling your strings lately? Are you tired of dancing to somebody else's tune? Do you want to learn to think for yourself? Are you ready to show the world who you are and what you can do?

Turn the page and begin reading Chapter One.

CHAPTER ONE
DON'T BLAME ME!

Living in a family
Is tricky as can be;
Rules are made for everything
As far as I can see.

I get up in the morning
And go to bed at night,
And if I do things by the rules,
Then I come out all right.

I have to eat my spinach;
I have to make my bed.
I'm told to do all kinds of things—
Except to use my head.

I want to do it my way.
I want to spread my wings,
But my folks say, "Stop! Don't do that!
You'll only mess up things."

I think they must not trust me.
They won't give me a chance
To show them I must learn to walk
Before I try to dance.

They say I like to play around.
They think it cannot be
That I am able to assume
Responsibility.

I really want to show them,
I want to let them know
That the family they've created
Is a perfect place to grow.

I really want to find a way,
But it's pretty hard, you see,
For living in a family
Is tricky as can be.

WHAT IS A FAMILY?

Unless you are a hermit and live in a cave, you are part of a family group. Originally, a family meant all the people living together in the same house. Today, when you say, "Family," you can mean relatives who live together and relatives who live apart. You can also be talking about special people who seem very close to you, but are really not relatives at all.

"Aunt Marian and Uncle Bob have lived next door for years and years," Jessie explained to her friend, Sue. "They're really not my aunt and uncle at all, but they seem just like part of the family."

LIVING IN A FAMILY

Most of the time you probably feel good about your family. But sometimes your family can seem like a pain. This is the time when you think you would be better off by yourself (even though you know it isn't true).

Family members don't always agree, and they don't always like the same things. This is because each member is an individual with different likes and dislikes.

People, you see, are a little like icebergs. Only a small part shows, and the rest—the most important part—is beneath the surface.

Because you can't see inside the people in your family, you sometimes have trouble understanding what makes them act the way they do.

But even though you disagree with your family some of the time, you know you can count on them when you have a problem. You know they will love you, no matter what.

Members of happy families...

>CARE FOR EACH OTHER
>SHARE WITH EACH OTHER
>TEACH EACH OTHER
>RESPECT EACH OTHER
>...even when they don't agree.

RULES AND REGULATIONS

Living in a family and obeying its rules are part of growing up. So are becoming independent and making some rules of your own. Somewhere in between are rules that you can **negotiate**. When you negotiate, you have a chance to change things by talking them over. First, let's have a look at...

Rules You Have to Obey No Matter What. Sometimes these are called **house rules**. They are here to stay, no matter how you feel about them. Parents always seem to say, "These rules are for your own good."

1. **Manners** are the way you act toward other people. Good manners mean being considerate, thoughtful, and polite. The language of good manners is easy to learn, but sometimes hard to remember.
2. **Responsibilities** are things you have to do all by yourself. Everybody else in the family expects you to get these things done. If you don't, you usually get yelled at. Common responsibilities are things like:

GETTING UP IN THE MORNING
    and
GETTING READY FOR SCHOOL
    and
GETTING HOME ON TIME
    and
GETTING YOUR CHORES DONE
    and
GETTING YOUR HOMEWORK
FINISHED BEFORE YOU WATCH TV.

You may have other responsibilities such as:

TAKING CARE OF A YOUNGER
BROTHER OR SISTER
    or
TAKING OUT THE TRASH
    or
TAKING CARE OF THE DOG
    or
TAKING YOUR TURN IN THE KITCHEN.

Rules That You Can Negotiate. When you really feel that a rule is unfair or too strict or just needs changing, then it's time to talk. It's OK to let your family know that you are mad or sad or just plain upset about something. But it's not OK to be rude or quarrelsome about it.

When you don't think something is fair, do these things:

—Think about the problem.
—Try to see the other side.
—Tell someone how you feel.
—Suggest a plan.
—Be willing to discuss it.

Here's what Nicole Simpson did to negotiate her problem. Nicole's bedtime had been nine o'clock for two years, and she thought it was time for a change. All her friends had been kidding her about her "baby" bedtime. Last month she even had to miss a TV special that was a school assignment.

Nicole understood how her parents felt. After all, she had been quite sick when she was younger, and had needed a lot of rest. "But I'm not sick now," Nicole thought. "I'm old enough to stay up later."

She told her parents how she felt. "I'm a lot older now," she said, "and I'm certainly not sick. I do my chores at home, and I've been getting good grades at school. I'd really like to stay up an hour later, if that's OK."

Nicole didn't get everything she asked for, but she did get her bedtime changed to 9:30—which was better than before.

When you decide that you are ready to negotiate—when you really want to make a change—you can be like Nicole.

DON'T WAIT.
THINK STRAIGHT.
MAKE A DATE
   to
COMMUNICATE!

MAKING SOME RULES OF YOUR OWN
Making rules of your own means pulling your own strings. If you think you are ready to give it a try, ask yourself these questions first:

1. **Am I reliable?** (Reliability means that people can depend on you to do what you promise to do. They can count on you to keep your word.)
2. **Do I tell the truth?** (Can you tell it the way it really is—without twisting the facts to suit yourself?)
3. **Do I know how to follow instructions?** (This can mean obeying orders, too.)

If you can answer yes to all three questions, you have learned a lot about self-discipline and responsibility, and you are ready to make a few rules of your own. Here are some areas you might want to consider:

PRIVACY

Everybody needs some of this. You have the right to ask that people knock on your bedroom door before they barge in on you. You have the right to be alone with your thoughts, but privacy is a privilege as well as a right. You can lose it if you abuse it.

FEELINGS

You are entitled to your own opinion. You have the right to ask your family to listen to your point of view. When they are considerate enough to do this, you should be willing to listen to them in return.

COMMUNICATIONS

You have the right to think what you like. However, you do not have the right to hurt other people's feelings. Here is a good rule to make for yourself: When you have a nice thought about someone, speak up. Share the good news! Give a compliment. Say thanks. Give credit when it's due. The rest of the time, keep your thoughts to yourself.

SHARING

You have a right to your own possessions. You don't like it when someone borrows without asking. Of course, **you** would never borrow without asking either! But when someone does ask, sharing is a generous thing to do, and it makes you feel good all over.

PRACTICALITIES

If you're a responsible person, you have the right to make some choices, such as...

HOW TO SPEND YOUR OWN MONEY
WHAT CLOTHES TO WEAR TO SCHOOL
WHETHER OR NOT YOU LIKE LIVER AND ONIONS
HOW TO WEAR YOUR HAIR
WHOM TO CHOOSE FOR FRIENDS
WHAT KIND OF MUSIC YOU LIKE
and MANY MORE....

Pulling your own strings means having a lot of rights and privileges—

and a lot of responsibilities, too!

Living in a family is the best way to learn how to grow up. It does not always mean getting your own way. It does not always mean being first. But it does mean being an independent, thoughtful person—somebody who is willing to take the responsibility for his or her own actions.

> Living in a family
> Is as tricky as can be,
> But it never, never, never means
> Don't blame me!

CHAPTER TWO
JOIN THE CLUB

I am a part of all I have met.
—Tennyson

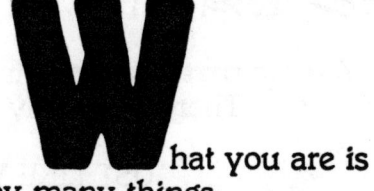

What you are is determined by many things:

YOU & YOUR FAMILY
YOUR FRIENDS
YOUR TOWN
YOUR COUNTRY
and YOUR EXPERIENCES:

SCHOOL
SWIMMING
CHURCH
CAMPING
LAWN MOWING

You are part of all you have met, but you are one of a kind. There is nobody else in the whole world

JUST LIKE YOU!

Because you are different, you have different ideas. Sometimes you even see things differently from the way other people do. This **Whatz-It Test** will show you just how different your vision can be.

INSTRUCTIONS:
1. Find a friend who'll take the test with you.
2. Find papers and pencils.
3. Look at the drawings and decide what they look like to you and your friend (but don't tell each other).

4. Write down your answers separately.
5. Compare your results.
   (Possible answers are at the end of this chapter.)

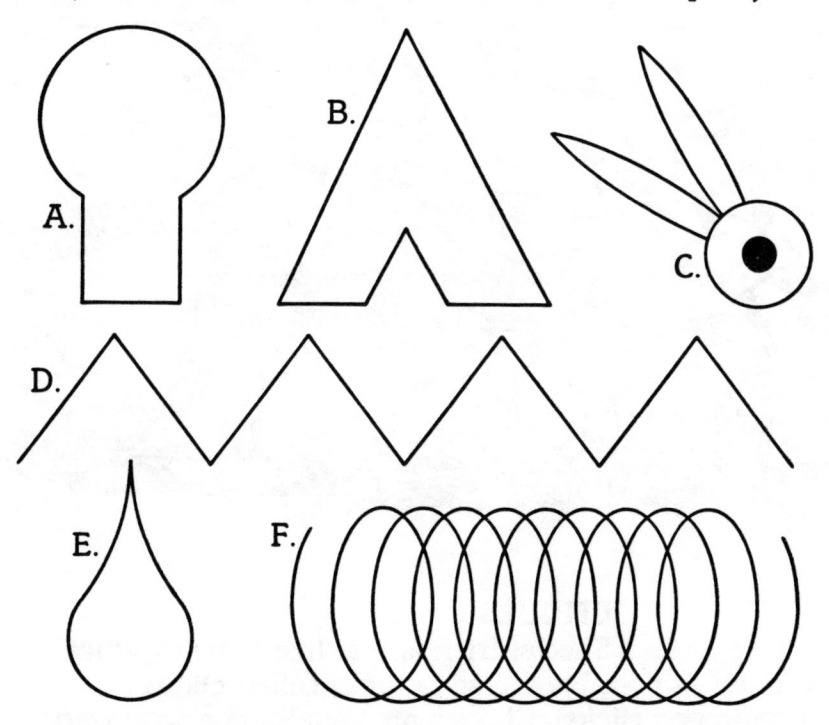

It is a fact that no two people ever think the same way about everything. But you and your friends probably like lots of the same things. You might...

> like the same music
> like the same people
> like the same sports
> like to wear the same clothes.

You even might.

> go to school
> and church
> and the beach—
> > together.

CLIQUES

Special friends that like to be together as much as possible are sometimes called **cliques** (pronounced **clicks**). Cliques are usually not organized groups. The members like to do things on the spur of the moment. They like to have fun together.

CLUBS

When people meet together regularly with a common purpose (they are all interested in the same thing), their group is called a **club**. There are all kinds of clubs. In your school, you might find clubs for

ART FANS
MUSIC FANS
STAMP COLLECTORS
BOOK LOVERS
SCIENCE FICTION FANS

Or you can start your own private clubs for anything you want, such as:

BIKING
HIKING
BIRD-WATCHING
  or even...
TV.

GANGS
Gangs are like big cliques. They are usually neighborhood kids who hang out together. Gang members like to dress the same way, act the same way, and talk the same way. They usually seem to think the same way.

Cliques, clubs, and **gangs** are all words with a plus (+). They mean YOU + OTHER PEOPLE. If you join a club or if you are part of a clique or a gang, you are an **insider.** You are part of the group. You belong.

Cliques, clubs, and **gangs** are words with an extra plus when they care about people and things outside their own groups.

Cliques, clubs, and **gangs** can also be words with a minus (−) because they mean YOU minus OTHER

PEOPLE. If you can't join a club or if you are kept from being part of a clique or a gang, you are an **outsider.** You are not part of the group. You don't belong.

Gloria Gonzalez was new in her neighborhood. Her parents didn't speak English very well, and Gloria felt anxious about making new friends. But on her first day in math class, she sat next to Tammie Fitzgerald.

"Hi," Tammie said. "Didn't I see you this morning coming out of that new apartment house on Seventh and Vine?"

Gloria nodded.

"Well, gee whiz," Tammie continued, "I live just down the street. A few other girls are coming over to play records after school. Why don't you come, too?"

Gloria hesitated, then smiled. "I'd like that—if you're sure it's OK."

It was OK. Tammie's friends made Gloria feel welcome and comfortable. She didn't have to feel anxious about living in a new neighborhood anymore.

Tammie's group was a clique with a **plus.** The members didn't shut people out.

Some cliques, clubs, and gangs are tight little groups that turn their backs on strangers. A group of girls like that gathered on the front steps of Central Junior High School every day. They laughed and talked among themselves. But whenever anyone new tried to join them, they whispered and looked the other way.

This kind of group is a group with a **minus** because the members shut people out. If you want to think for yourself, these "minus" groups are not for you.

> It's OK to choose your own friends.
> It's OK to like some people better than others.
> It's not OK to let your group do your thinking for you.

Cliques, clubs, and **gangs** are words with an extra

minus when they keep people out because of race, skin color, and/or religion, or when they harm people or things outside their own groups.

Some groups, such as street gangs, can cause a lot of trouble when the members act tough, break the law, or threaten other people.

WHY JOIN?

You might want to join a clique, club, or gang for these reasons:

1. **To have fun.** It's natural to want to have fun. It's good to enjoy the company of people you like. Members of happy groups make plans together, laugh a lot, and look forward to the next get-together.
2. **To make friends.** It's natural to want to have friends. Close friends share ideas and thoughts. Friends can help you when you feel lonely or when you have a problem. They can laugh with you when you're glad.
3. **To banish boredom.** It's natural to feel bored now and then, but nobody enjoys the feeling. Being part of a group can help you feel **interested** and **enthusiastic**. When you can talk to people who like the same things you do, it's hard to be bored.
4. **To use your talents.** It's natural to want to do what you do best. It makes you feel good when your friends appreciate your abilities.
5. **To find direction.** When you have to make a decision, it's good to talk to friends. They can support you, give advice to you, or just listen to you.

WHAT TO DO
BEFORE YOU JOIN ANY GROUP
1. Find out what the members like to do.
2. Get acquainted with each person.

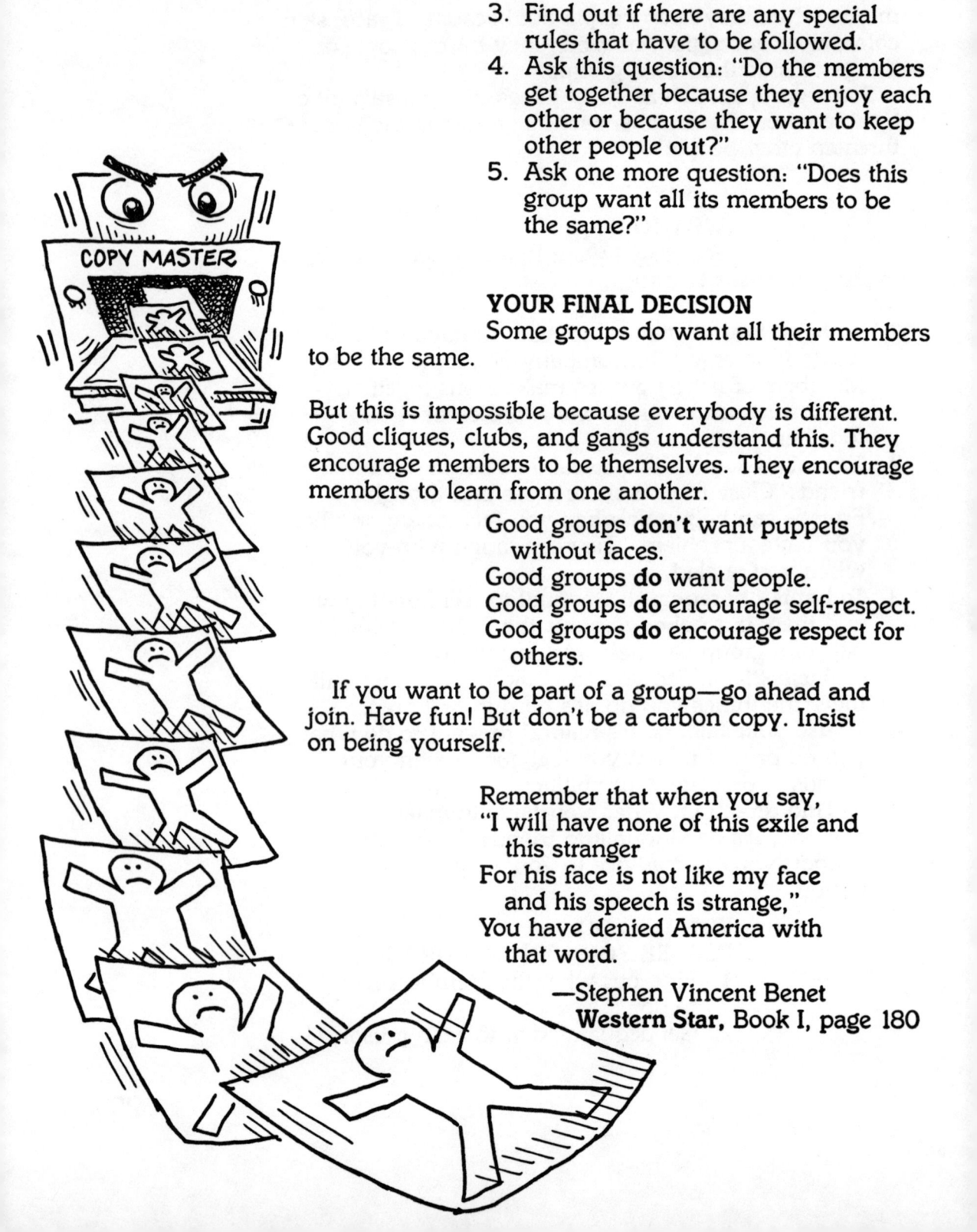

3. Find out if there are any special rules that have to be followed.
4. Ask this question: "Do the members get together because they enjoy each other or because they want to keep other people out?"
5. Ask one more question: "Does this group want all its members to be the same?"

YOUR FINAL DECISION
Some groups do want all their members to be the same.

But this is impossible because everybody is different. Good cliques, clubs, and gangs understand this. They encourage members to be themselves. They encourage members to learn from one another.

> Good groups **don't** want puppets without faces.
> Good groups **do** want people.
> Good groups **do** encourage self-respect.
> Good groups **do** encourage respect for others.

If you want to be part of a group—go ahead and join. Have fun! But don't be a carbon copy. Insist on being yourself.

> Remember that when you say,
> "I will have none of this exile and this stranger
> For his face is not like my face and his speech is strange,"
> You have denied America with that word.
>
> —Stephen Vincent Benet
> **Western Star,** Book I, page 180

Answers to WHATZ-IT TEST (all answers are correct ones)

A. mushroom
tree
chef's hat
light bulb
hot-air balloon
flower vase turned upside down
B. tepee
the letter **A**
an inverted **V**
an Indian arrowhead with a chip
out of it
a cowboy without a horse
C. rabbit
duck
last two petals of a daisy
D. mountain peaks
lightning striking sideways
closeup of a dinosaur's back
saw blade
E. teardrop
candle flame
polliwog
a fat comma
F. coiled spring
caterpillar
long tail of a pig
a Slinky toy
squiggles

CHAPTER THREE
PROMISES...PROMISES

The head bone's connected to the
 neck bone...
Now hear the Word of the Lord.

—Old folk song

It's no accident that your head is right up there on top of the rest of you. It's the best possible arrangement. You can see better, hear better, smell better, breathe better, and think better this way. At least, you can when your head is screwed on straight.

Unfortunately, when you refuse to use your thinking machine the way it was meant to be used, there are people around who are waiting to step in and do your thinking for you. It's a sad fact that some of these are very dangerous people who pretend that they want to help you in the name of their "lord."

These people are master string-pullers—cult leaders who are always on the lookout for new puppets to manipulate.

WHAT IS A CULT?

A **cult** is a group of people who live together and practice their own religion. A cult has unorthodox (unusual) religious beliefs and practices. Sometimes members must shave their heads and wear strange clothes. Sometimes they must eat only certain foods. Members of a cult have a strong dedication to their leader—so strong, in fact, that the leader often calls himself "prophet," "messiah," or even "god."

The cult leader makes all the rules, and they must be followed without question. The leader usually lives in luxury, while the cult members do all the hard work.

When a person joins a cult, he or she must give up everything—job, possessions, friends, and family. People in cults are taught that they are better than other people and that they are the only ones who know the "TRUTH."

They are brainwashed into believing "Do as you are told, and everything will be all right." People who belong to cults are not allowed to think for themselves. After a while, they don't even know that they are acting like zombies.*

WHY DOES ANYONE JOIN A CULT?

When a person is unhappy or sad or discontented or confused, he or she is **vulnerable**. This means that the unhappy person is sensitive and easily influenced.

Cults are always on the lookout for unhappy or confused people, and always offer to help them. Cults will promise anything to get you to join.

*zombie: an old voodoo word that describes a dead body walking around.

WHAT DO CULTS PROMISE?
1. Cults may promise freedom from responsibility. What they don't tell you is . . . you won't have anything to be responsible for.
2. Cults may tell you that you will never have to worry about money again. What they don't tell you is . . . you won't have any to worry about.
3. Cults may promise you a new family. What they don't tell you is . . . you must give up your old family and all your old friends.
4. Cults may promise you a new identity. What they don't tell you is . . . you were better off the way you were.
5. Cults always promise you something to believe in. What they don't tell you is . . . your opinion doesn't count.

HOW TO RECOGNIZE A CULT
A cult never calls itself a cult. Instead, it uses titles that promise LOVE, LIFE, TRUTH, FULFILLMENT, and KNOWLEDGE.

But so do a lot of worthwhile organizations. Then how do you recognize a cult when you see one? Here are some basic danger signals to look for.

1. **Recruiting.** Cults invite people to meetings without telling them what the meetings are really about. Cult members treat newcomers as if they are the most special people they have ever met.
2. **Daydreaming.** Cults talk about what they are going to do, but can never tell you what they have done.
3. **Isolating.** Cults require your complete attention. You must give up all other relationships.
4. **Following.** Cults always follow a leader who says he is showing them the **"New Way."** They must believe everything he says.
5. **Criticizing.** Cults are opposed to regular churches. They always claim to have discovered the Truth, the Way, or the Light...and they say that nobody else knows what it is.

6. **Capturing.** Cults make it very easy for you to join them, but almost impossible for you to leave.

THE HIGH COST OF CULTING

Cults like to tell you that admission is free. What they don't tell you is. . .you are getting a free ticket to nowhere. When you set out to find yourself—and join a cult—you end up losing yourself, as well as

    YOUR FAMILY
    YOUR FRIENDS
    YOUR FUTURE
      and
    YOUR POTENTIAL.

Things are not always what they seem;
Don't be dazzled, as if in a dream.

Examine the facts, and use your head;
Consider the evidence—don't be led.

Then when it's time to make a choice,
You'll speak right up, with a good,
    strong voice.

Don't be a zombie; don't be a sap;
Don't fall into the cultist trap.

CHAPTER FOUR
A REAL HIGH

Josh stuffed both hands into his pockets, clenched his fists, and waited for his father to finish.

"Those kids you're running around with are a bunch of bums, Josh. Pretty soon you're going to be just like them—smoking, drinking, and..."

"Wait a minute, Dad," Josh interrupted. "Those guys are my friends. They're real cool. Anyway, you don't have to worry about me. I'm old enough to make my own decisions."

Josh is fifteen, and he is right about one thing. It's time for him to start making decisions. What Josh doesn't seem to realize is that the choices he makes today will affect the rest of his life.

Josh is no different from anyone else. He wants to be happy. He wants to feel good, and he wants people to feel good about him. When this happens, Josh is on top of the world. He has a really "high" feeling.

GETTING HIGH

There's nothing the matter with getting high. It's a great, big, wonderful feeling. You can get high on:

LOVE
FRIENDSHIP
LAUGHTER
WORK
RECREATION
SCHOOL
NATURE
RELIGION
MUSIC
BOOKS
HOBBIES.

"Feeling high" means feeling good in a special way—physically, mentally, emotionally, and spiritually. It is the kind of feeling that you wish could last forever.

COUNTERFEIT HIGHS

There is nothing more worthless than a seven-dollar bill. Everyone knows it's not real. A counterfeit high is a lot like counterfeit money. It doesn't do you any good at all.

As a matter of fact, it can do you a lot of harm. A counterfeit high is not natural. It is a false feeling of well-being. It never lasts. It is a poor substitute for the real thing.

Counterfeit highs come when people smoke, drink,

inhale, inject, or swallow harmful substances. They are trying to feel good, but all they get is:

>BOMBED
>BLACKED OUT
>ZONKED
>BUZZED
>STONED
>FREAKED OUT
>or
>WIRED.

**HARMFUL WAYS
PEOPLE TRY TO GET HIGH**

1. **Nicotine.** Nicotine is a poison found in tobacco leaves. It is often used as an insecticide to kill harmful bugs. When a person smokes tobacco, the effect can be the same as that of an insecticide. The poisonous nicotine goes right to work, causing heart disease, lung disease, and cancer.

    If slow death is not enough to keep you away from nicotine, you might consider that **smoking is a dirty habit.** Why?

It stains your teeth and fingers.
It gives you bad breath.
It fouls the air around you.

2. **Alcohol.** Alcohol is strong enough to kill germs. It can make a racing car go 200 miles per hour. If you light alcohol with a match, it will burn. It is a powerful chemical that should be treated with respect. When misused, alcohol can make you very sick or even kill you. The amount of alcohol in just one bottle of beer will:

   —dull your senses of taste and smell
   —relax your eye muscles so that it is hard to focus on what you want to see
   —make your arms and legs feel floppy
   —blur your speech
   —change your mood.

3. **Drugs.** Barbiturates, tranquilizers, narcotics, amphetamines, and hallucinogens are all drugs. Some slow you down. Some speed you up. Some put you to sleep. Some make you think you can fly. Some make you see things that aren't there.

   A few are useful when prescribed by doctors.
   All are very dangerous when prescribed by yourself!
   Drugs can be killers. They are **addictive.**

Addiction means "to be enslaved and taken over by a master." When drugs are your master, it's tough to escape. People who take drugs and think they feel high, have to take more and more drugs to avoid feeling low.

You don't have to be "under the influence" to be hurt by smoking, drinking, or by using drugs.

Statistics show that just being near someone who is smoking is harmful to your health because you are breathing the air that he has polluted.

Getting into a car with a person who has been drinking or taking drugs is not simply harmful to your health—it can kill you.

4. **Gluttony.** This is another common problem that might surprise you. Gluttony is a type of greed. It means gulping down more food than your body needs. Some people get their highs by overeating. They don't know when to stop. The problem is that they feel high only when they are chewing. The rest of the time they don't feel very good about themselves.

Brenda is addicted to food, and she is getting fatter and fatter. One day Jack saw her as she was stuffing a big piece of chocolate cake into her mouth.

"Why do you eat so much, Brenda?" he asked.

Brenda's eyes seemed to bulge as she answered, "Because it makes me feel so good."

Too much weight is dangerous to Brenda's health. It keeps her body from working properly. Besides, it keeps her from looking her best. Brenda is really a very unhappy person. When she isn't eating, she doesn't feel good about herself at all.

Almost everybody likes to eat. Most people have favorite foods they really enjoy. But when you get your jollies from overeating, you are getting a counterfeit high.

Everybody wants to feel happy. Everybody wants to feel good. But counterfeit highs are not the answer. Cigarettes, booze, and drugs are available to anyone who wants to look for them. But there's a better way—one that will never let you down.

A REAL HIGH

The following method costs you nothing more than five minutes of your time. The more you practice, the better you will get. Here's how you can go about getting a REAL HIGH.

1. **Find a place where you can sit down.** Outside is best. If you can't go outside, then sit by an open window. Sit on anything—even an old sweater on the grass—but **don't lie down.**

2. **Close your eyes.** Really close them. Don't worry about people staring at you. You can't see them unless you are cheating. Don't blink. Don't flutter. Just relax. You are going to stay like this for five whole minutes. Look at the darkness. Try to enjoy it. Don't peek, or you will blow the whole thing. Now...

3. **Listen carefully.** Concentrate on the sounds you hear. What are they? When your eyes are open, you depend on your sight. When you close them, your hearing seems to get better. You will hear sounds you weren't aware of a few seconds before: voices, doors closing, perhaps a radio playing. Or the sound of wind in the trees and the chattering of birds. Hold on to those sounds while you begin to...

4. **Feel.** Start with the tips of your toes and work your way up. Feel your shoes against your feet, your clothes against your body. Hold up your hand and feel the breeze blowing soft air against your skin. Let the sun warm your face. Don't stop. You're coming alive! In a few seconds you will be ready to use your sense of...

5. **Smell.** Take three deep breaths. Breathe in slowly and evenly through your nose. Let the air go all the way down to the pit of your stomach. Hold it

to the count of five and let it out slowly through your mouth. Can you smell a cake baking or flowers blooming? Can you smell freshly cut grass or hot concrete?

6. **Now lick your lips.** What did you taste? Nothing? Try again. Did you know that you can actually taste things that you haven't put into your mouth? You can sometimes taste through smelling—as when you walk past a bakery shop early in the morning and smell fresh doughnuts. You can almost taste them, can't you?

How do you feel when Thanksgiving dinner is in the oven? It smells so good that you can almost taste it. Taste is a lot more than telling the difference between foods. It is the ability to **appreciate**. Lick your lips one more time. Are you beginning to taste the joy of being alive?

7. **Your five minutes are up. Very slowly open your eyes.** Look around you. You're in for a surprise. Because your other senses are still busily working, you are now seeing with more than your eyes. Everything is sharply in focus. The colors are so vivid that you can almost taste the green of the trees and smell the blue sky. The effect can sometimes be so startling that you feel the need to blink and look again.

You are as high as a kite, and you got there under your own steam. You are on top of the world. If you follow these steps to get there, you will never come down.

CHAPTER FIVE
SEEING STARS: HOROSCOPES, CRYSTAL BALLS, AND OTHER FORTUNE COOKIES

Buzz Evans wants to find out what the future holds for him. The trouble is that he doesn't know what to believe.

His newspaper horoscope says, "Romance is on the way." His fortune cookie tells him, "Man with many girl friends soon has empty rice bowl." The coin-operated weight machine down on the corner warns him: "Beware of new relationships."

Buzz is no different from anyone else. He is curious about tomorrow.

Tomorrow is a mysterious word. Everybody knows what happened yesterday. Everybody knows what is happening today. But what about the future? The future is a kind of unknown land where anything can happen.

BUT WHAT?

For thousands of years, that is exactly what people have been trying to find out. All sorts of questions have been asked about the future. Here are some that you might be asking about your own future:

> Will I be rich?
> Will I be famous?
> Will my face ever clear up?
> Will I pass math?
> Will I travel?
> Will my little sister/brother ever stop bugging me?
> When will I have my own wheels?

Throughout history, certain people have tried to figure out what might happen in the future. Because they used many different methods, they were called by many different names. Some of these names are tricky to spell and difficult to pronounce, but they are all fun to read about.

Astrologers (uh-strah́-luh-gers)* believe that heavenly bodies affect our lives. Their predictions are called **horoscopes.** These are based upon what the stars and planets were doing when you were born.

Today, you can find daily horoscopes printed in many newspapers. They are a little like Chinese fortune cookies—fun to read, but not very believable.

Cartomancers (cár-toe-man-sirs) are people who try to tell fortunes by using special decks of cards. The profession of cartomancy started way back in the Middle Ages when people were willing to believe all kinds of silly things.

Chiromancers (kí-row-man-sirs) are people who believe that the lines on your hands can tell all about you and predict your future. Because chiromancers study your palms, they are called **palmists** or **palm readers.** Today, people often dress up as gypsy fortune-tellers at

*****Astrologers** and **astronomers** are not the same kinds of people. An astronomer is a scientist who studies the heavens to find out more about them, not to foretell the future.

Halloween parties and pretend to read palms just for fun. They say things like:

> "You are going on a long ocean voyage."
> "I see a tall, handsome stranger in your future."
> "You are going to be rich and famous."

Crystal-gazers are fortune-tellers who gaze into glass balls and pretend to see pictures of future events. Crystal-gazers have good imaginations, but they are not very dependable. If the glass breaks, they are out of business.

Diviners (dee-viné-urs) are also called **haruspices** (ha-rooś-puh-sees). These are people who claim to see the future by studying the entrails (insides) of sacrificed animals. This sounds like a rather gruesome sport, especially for the animals. Fortunately, civilized countries don't allow animals to be sacrificed anymore.

Geomancers (geé-uh-man-sirs) are people who throw handfuls of dirt onto the ground. Then they look at the mess they've made and predict the future from it. Geomancers make poor houseguests, because they leave dirt behind them wherever they go.

Phrenologists (freh-nah-luh-gists) are people who say they can tell all about you and your abilities by feeling the bumps on your head. To a phrenologist, life really has its ups and downs. He is especially interested in people who have had one hard knock after another.

Physiognomists (fizz-ee-og-nuh-mists) are people who claim to know all about you and your abilities by studying your facial features. They spend a lot of time measuring the length of your nose and the distance between your eyes. They also like foreheads, chins, and cheekbones.

People have also tried to predict the future by studying things like:

> STICKS, SEEDS, RIVERS, BONES, RAIN, TREES, STONES, WATER, AIR, FIRE, HANDWRITING, OUIJA BOARDS,
>   and even...
> TEA LEAVES!

People have wasted a lot of time trying to figure out what tomorrow will bring. The truth is... there is no way of knowing. The only thing you can deal with is today—and today is the fabric of tomorrow.

> What you do today... **COUNTS**.
> What you do today... **MATTERS**.

Take care of today,
   and
tomorrow will take care of itself.

Therefore do not be anxious about tomorrow, for tomorrow will be anxious for itself. Let the day's own trouble be sufficient for the day.

—Matthew 6:34 RSV

CHAPTER SIX
AND NOW, A WORD FROM OUR SPONSORS...

Have you ever seen a good fly fisherman at work? (**Flies** are those colorful, feathery lures that a fisherman uses for bait.) A fly fisherman casts his lure into the water, hoping that the fish will see it and think it is a bug. If one lure doesn't work, he tries another. He may change his lure many times in one morning until he finally hooks a fish.

A good fly fisherman is a lot like a good advertising man. They both use bait skillfully. But instead of flies, the advertising man uses psychology. This means that he tries to find out what makes you want to buy his products. Then he creates appealing advertisements and dangles them in front of you until you snap at the bait... and buy.

Clever advertising can make you want to be:

> MORE ATTRACTIVE
> MORE POPULAR
> MORE MATURE
> MORE IMPORTANT
> HAPPIER
> SMARTER
> SHAPELIER
> SEXIER
>   and
> HEALTHIER.

Clever ads can make you hungry and thirsty. They can even make your mouth water.

Advertising has been around a long time. The early Babylonians wrote advertising messages on large flat tablets made out of clay. In Greece, the advertisements were shouted in the streets by special men called **town criers**. The Egyptians wrote their ads on pieces of papyrus. In ancient Pompeii, directions to shops were chiseled into the stone streets, and signs were often painted on the walls. In England, some of the first advertisements were wooden signs attached to the walls of inns. These stuck out over the roads to draw attention.

Today's world is full of advertising. In modern Hong Kong, the streets are filled with so many signs that sometimes it is difficult to see the buildings.

>Advertising can be interesting.
>Advertising can be informative.
>Advertising can be entertaining.

But advertising can also be **overwhelming**. And sometimes it can be **misleading**. If you take all the bait that is offered, you might find yourself wanting things that you don't need. You might find yourself buying things that you don't really want (and maybe can't afford).

Here's what happened to a boy named Phil when he listened to all the advertisements without using good judgment.

"I'm ready. Let's get going," Phil said as he stood in Jack's front yard, panting heavily. Sweat was running down his flushed cheeks.

Jack stared at him. "I thought we were going on an all-day hike. You look as if you're packed for moving to Siberia. What are you carrying all that junk for, anyway?"

Phil looked surprised. "These are just the bare necessities. We're going to need every bit of this stuff. Look. I'll show you what I brought."

55

Phil pointed to his new utility belt. "This holds my eight-bladed camping knife, a compass, a first-aid kit, a hatchet, a flashlight, and a canteen."

He gestured toward his backpack. "In here I have a water distillation kit, my Boy Scout manual, a rope, a walkie-talkie, a signaling mirror, some spare socks, a swimsuit, and my pajamas."

Jack snorted. "Your pajamas!"

Phil nodded and smiled happily. "And in this roll is a two-man pup tent and a sleeping bag."

Jack sighed and shook his head. "Hey, man, all we're gonna do is climb the hill behind your house. I have to be home in time for dinner."

"That's not the point," Phil insisted. "You have to be prepared. Haven't you seen the camping ads?"

"Yeah, I've seen them," Jack answered, "but, gee whiz, Phil! You have to use a little common sense. By the way, what did you bring for lunch?"

Phil looked embarrassed. "Uh, I was so busy packing, I guess I forgot."

Poor gullible Phil has fallen into the advertising trap. He took all the bait that was offered and swallowed it right down.

The same thing can happen to you. Clever advertising can make you believe that beauty aids, clothes, games, mouthwash, soap, deodorant, soft drinks, motorcycles, and music will make you

>HEALTHY
>WEALTHY
> and
>WISE
> or
>whatever else you want to be!

Turning on the TV or the radio, opening a magazine or a newspaper, looking at billboards, walking through the supermarket, or just opening the mail can get you into a lot of trouble if you don't use your head.

Before you decide to spend your money on any product, you might want to ask yourself some of these questions:

1. Do I really want this product?
2. Do I really need this product?
3. Can I afford to buy it?
4. Will I have to buy something else to make it work right? (Extra parts? Batteries?)
5. Will I use it a lot?
6. Will it improve me or make me feel good about myself?
7. Will it last as long as it is supposed to?
8. Does it have a money-back guarantee?
9. Will it be out of style soon?

If the product is a food, ask yourself:

1. Is it full of empty calories?
2. Is it classified as "junk food"?
3. Will it make my skin break out?
4. Will it make me fat?

All you have to do now is DECIDE FOR YOURSELF. Making decisions for yourself is part of growing up. It isn't always easy. Sometimes it seems like a lot of work. Occasionally, you will make a mistake. But deciding for yourself is the best way in the world to pull your own strings.

> Don't be swayed
> And don't act nervous;
> Weigh the facts—
> You'll be impervious.

> Avoid the bait
> That's offered each day,
> And you'll be the fish
> That got away.

> Just use your head.
> Don't be a sap,
> And you'll escape
> The advertising trap!

CHAPTER SEVEN
MANNERS THAT MATTER

Manners are the happy ways of doing things.

—Ralph Waldo Emerson

Once upon a time, in an ordinary town, on an ordinary street, in an ordinary house, there lived an ordinary family with one exception. Herman.

Herman's father and mother and sister, Angela, were perfectly nice people. But Herman wasn't. He was rude, dirty, and mean. His only companion was his dog, Termite, who was a lot like Herman. Termite was dirty. His coat was all matted and full of burrs. Besides that, Termite had a short temper and was full of fleas.

Angela looked at Herman one day

and said, "Herman, you make me sick. Why are you such a slob?"

Herman glared at his sister. "What do you mean by that?"

"Well, just look at yourself," she said. "You are filthy. You have bad manners. And you like to act mean."

Herman puffed himself up until the dust rose in the air around him.

"Well," Angela insisted, "answer me! Why are you such a slob?"

Herman stood up and shook his fist in Angela's face. "Because that's the way I choose to be!" he yelled. Then he kicked Angela in the shin and stalked out of the room. Termite followed him, growling.

A few days later, Herman's mother came into his room and sat down carefully on the edge of his bed.

"Herman," she said, "this room is not safe for human habitation. I've told you a hundred times to pick up all this junk. Your friends have stopped coming over, and I don't blame them. The only thing that wants to come in here is that dog of yours, that Termite. Listen, Herman, both of you need to take a bath."

Herman looked at the floor and cracked his knuckles awhile. "I'm allergic to soap," he finally muttered. Then he glanced over at his dog. "I'm afraid to give him a bath. I think he might sprout."

"Don't you try to be sassy with me, young man. Just wait until your father gets home!" Herman's mother went out of the room and slammed the door behind her.

Herman ran his hand over Termite's matted ears. Termite growled. "Don't worry," Herman told him. "She's just a mother. She doesn't scare us."

When Herman's father came home, he put a handkerchief over his nose and went to look for Herman.

"This has gone far enough," he announced. "It's time you changed your ways. You are rude to your mother, mean to your sister, and you don't care how you look.

People are staying away from you, Herman. You might as well live in a cave and be a hermit."

"That's OK with me." Herman laughed loudly. "A hermit is a spicy cookie—with nuts and raisins and good stuff in it."

His father sighed. "The only spicy thing about you is the way you smell. Herman, you have to take a bath. NOW!"

Herman looked his father in the eye. "I won't," he said. Termite growled low in his throat.

Herman's father looked right back at him and said a surprising thing. "OK, Herman. That's all right with me. You can be rude, mean, and dirty, if that's the way you want it. But you'll have to stay in your room where you won't bother anybody else."

Herman's father went out of the room and slammed the door behind him. Termite growled again. "Don't worry," Herman muttered. "He's just a father. He doesn't scare us."

Herman started to read a comic book, but he couldn't seem to concentrate. Then he tried to find his favorite mind-bender puzzle, but is was somewhere under all the mess. He turned on his radio, but the battery was dead. All he could do was sit and watch Termite scratch his fleas.

Later, Herman could hear voices downstairs. He opened his door just a crack so he could hear them better. His sister, Angela, was laughing, and his mother and father were joining in. From the kitchen came wonderful, mouth-watering smells—much better than the smells in his bedroom.

Dinner came and went and nobody called Herman. It was almost bedtime when his mother knocked on the door. She was carrying a tray with a sandwich and a glass of milk. "We missed you at dinner, Herman," she said. Herman thought his mother looked sad. He pushed his hair nervously out of his eyes.

"It's kind of lonesome up here," he whispered.

His mother set the tray down and glanced around the room. "Oh, really?" She sounded surprised. "But, Herman, you have your books and games and your dog, Termite. What else could a boy ask for?"

Herman cleared his throat. His voice sounded squeaky when he said, "People. There aren't any people up here."

"The world is full of people," his mother said. "But people don't like to be teased or mocked or punched or kicked or, uh, offended." She put her hand quickly over her nose. "Herman, can't you see that no one is going to like you unless you make yourself likable?"

Herman pushed his hair out of his eyes again. "But I don't know how."

"You can start with good manners, Herman. Good manners are just thoughtful ways of doing things.

People with good manners are not rude or mean, and, for starters, they take baths."

She went out and closed the door softly behind her. Herman stared at the door while he munched the sandwich. Then he cracked his knuckles until his hands got tired. Pretty soon he got up and began putting things away in his drawers.

"This is going to be a bigger job than I thought," he said to Termite.

Finally Herman opened the door and peeked out. Everybody in the family had gone to bed. "Come on, Termite," he whispered. And he tiptoed to the bathroom and began to fill the bathtub with water—for both of them.

The next morning Herman got up and looked at himself in the mirror. Termite sat on the floor and whimpered. "It's all right, boy," Herman said. "Everybody has to make sacrifices now and then."

He brushed his hair and Termite's, too. Then he looked for his missing shoelace and crawled under the bed to hunt for some clean clothes. Nobody called him to breakfast, but he could smell bacon and hot pancakes.

At first, nobody said a word when Herman slipped into his place at the table. Then his sister asked, "Who let in that strange dog?"

"That's Termite," Herman told her. "He's not strange—he's just clean. We, uh, had a bath last night, and that's how he came out."

"Hmmm." His father smiled at him over the top of his newspaper. "You look a little different, too."

Herman's mother put a big platter of steaming pancakes on the table. "Oh, boy!" Herman exclaimed. He stood up and reached across the table, his fork leading the attack.

"Would you like someone to pass the pancakes, Herman?" his mother asked. Her voice had that kind of tone that always meant she was trying to tell him something.

"Uh, oh, yeah, sure," Herman muttered. He sat down and stabbed only three pancakes instead of the whole plateful. Then he looked around for the syrup. His sister, Angela, was using it.

"Gimme that!" he yelled and cocked his foot to kick her under the table. Termite growled softly. Herman caught himself just in time. "Easy, boy," he whispered. He put his foot back on the floor and forced himself to look pleasant.

"Pass the syrup," he said, "uh, please."

Angela looked startled and handed it to him quickly. "Thanks," he murmured.

Angela's mouth was hanging open. "You're welcome," she managed to say.

Herman's father put his paper down. "What are your plans for today, Herman?"

Herman thought about that. It was Saturday. He could play baseball with the guys. He could go fishing in the river. He could even take Termite and go down to the dump and dig awhile. Herman looked at his father and swallowed hard. "I have to finish cleaning my room," he said.

The room was very quiet. Then Herman's mother carried another big plate of steaming pancakes over to the table. "You look hungry this morning, Herman," she said. "Why don't you finish up this plateful while I make some more?"

Herman sniffed the pancakes. They smelled wonderful. He poured syrup over the top and took a big bite. **It takes a lot of self-control to have good manners,** Herman thought. He swallowed and took another bite. His mother and his father and his sister, Angela, smiled.

Herman realized it was worth it.

It was a lot easier on Herman when he chose to act civilized. Being civilized means having good manners. Good manners are nothing more than thoughtful—happy—ways of doing things.

When you show that you care about other people, other people show that they care about you—and the world is a happier place for everyone.

The way you act is your choice. Sometimes it takes a lot of self-control to have good manners, but as Herman found out, it is definitely worth it.

> Hearts, like doors, will open with ease
> To very, very little keys,
> And don't forget that two of these
> Are "I thank you" and "If you please."
> —Mother Goose

CHAPTER EIGHT
WHO'S THE MASTER OF YOUR FATE?

Action may not always bring happiness, but there is no happiness without action.

—Disraeli

If you are a recently liberated puppet on a string, you probably have a lot of loose ends. Maybe you need some help now that you are setting your own goals.

GOALS
Goals are **objectives**, the things you want to do in the future. Goals are what you aim at, and you want to hit the mark.

A poet named Longfellow once said:

I shot an arrow into the air.
It fell to earth, I knew not where.

The archer in the poem forgot where to point. He didn't even have an objective. What a waste of time and strength, not to mention the cost of a lost arrow.

When you aim **your** arrow—when **you** shoot for a goal—make sure you know where your target is. This is called **direction**.

Make sure you know why that particular target is important. This is called **purpose**.

Make sure you know how much strength to use. This is called **drive**.

Direction, purpose, and drive are all necessary. They are the three musketeers of ambition. They work together to help you reach your goal. Without them, your arrow will fall short.

There are two kinds of goals:

1. Short-term goals
2. Long-term goals.

Short-term goals are objectives that you can easily reach in a short length of time. Long-term goals are major projects. These take a longer time to reach and usually require more effort.

Jake wanted to build a radio-controlled model airplane. He figured it would take about six months to complete.

Jake's problem was that he couldn't afford to buy everything he needed at once. So he decided to take it one step at a time.

First, he bought the basic model kit and got started (short-term goal #1). By working after school at odd jobs, he was soon able to buy the radio-control equipment (short-term goal #2), and finally, an engine (short-term goal #3). At the end of six months, Jake had the radio-controlled model airplane that he had always wanted (long-term goal completed).

> When a long-term
> goal seems
> too faraway,
> remember that
> you can
> often reach
> it in
> easy steps.

Remember, too, that you will never get anywhere unless you put one foot in front of the other... and MOVE!

The following **Tie-Up-Your-Loose-Ends-Quiz** will show you whether **you** can stand on your own two feet. Circle only one answer; then read the evaluations that follow.

TIE UP YOUR LOOSE ENDS
1. When I have to make up my mind, I
   A. Ask my best friend to tell me what to do.
   B. Flip a coin.
   C. Investigate the problem and weigh the facts.

   EVALUATIONS: If you chose
   A. You are still dependent. You are allowing your best friend to pull your strings.
   B. You are in danger of becoming a two-bit gambler.
   C. Good decisions are made by using good judgment. Good judgment comes from good information. Good for you, if you chose this answer!

2. Do I know what I want to do with the rest of my life?
   A. Sometimes I think I want to do one thing, and sometimes another.
   B. I haven't the vaguest idea.
   C. My father hasn't decided yet.

   EVALUATIONS: If you chose
   A. It's OK to be undecided or to change your mind. You are thinking about what you want to do—and that's good.
   B. It's time to make a list. Write down:

      —five things that make you happy
      —five things that make you sad
      —five people you admire
      —five things you do well.

These will help you think about yourself.
C. It's good to listen to advice from your family. But the final decision has to be yours. Stop taking the easy way out!

3. What I think about daydreaming:
   A. Only a nerd does that.
   B. It's a good way to get through English.
   C. It's a good way to think quietly and get my thoughts together.

   EVALUATIONS: If you chose
   A. You are a practical, sensible person, but you need to relax and enjoy life.
   B. Daydreaming can be a good way to **flunk** English! You are trying to escape. This is not what daydreams are for.
   C. You've got the picture. Daydreaming lets your imagination go to work. It is creative. It can help you solve problems. Of course, daydreaming is good only in small doses.

4. When I have a chore to do, I
   A. Refuse to think about it and have a snack, so I won't get depressed.
   B. Look for the best way to do it and then finish it quickly so I can enjoy something else.
   C. Try to find someone to do it for me.

   EVALUATIONS: If you chose
   A. You are acting like an ostrich hiding its head in the sand. Running away from responsibility doesn't solve a thing.
   B. Give yourself a pat on the back. You

are the kind of person who knows how to tackle everyday problems.
C. You may be a good organizer, but you will soon be out of friends.

5. During summer vacation, I like to
   A. Just sit back and watch TV.
   B. Do the things I never have time for, such as: swimming, hiking, reading, listening to music, cooking, drawing, biking, and having fun with my family and friends.
   C. Work at odd jobs (such as yard work, washing cars, cleaning house, and baby-sitting) to earn spending money.

   EVALUATIONS: If you chose
   A. Remember that someone else is doing all your chores while you act like royalty. It's fun to watch TV for a while, but nobody should become addicted to it.
   B. You are a winner. You are using your spare time for constructive activities. But don't forget to take care of your responsibilities while you are having a good time.
   C. Another winner. You are responsible and conscientious. Don't forget, however, that "all work and **no** play make Jack a dull boy."

6. When my class has a meeting, I
   A. Try to vote with the side that is going to win.
   B. Listen to all the arguments before deciding.
   C. Make up my mind and refuse to change it.

   EVALUATIONS: If you chose
   A. Going along with the crowd seems like an easy way out, but it doesn't

always make sense. If the crowd decides to go to a fire walker's convention, are you willing to walk barefoot through the coals with your friends?
B. Congratulations. You are pulling your own strings. You may or may not win, but you are giving it your best shot.
C. People who won't change their minds are **inflexible**. This means they won't bend. Everyone knows what happens to a tree that won't bend in the wind. It gets blown to the ground.

7. When I get called on in class,
   A. I am not surprised, because my teacher has got it in for me.
   B. I may get sweaty palms, and my voice may crack, but I go ahead and answer the best I can.
   C. I ask the teacher if I can be excused because I suddenly feel sick.

   EVALUATIONS: If you chose
   A. Teachers rarely pick on students. Could it be that you are so touchy because you are not prepared?
   B. Everyone gets nervous sometimes, but you stand up and do your thing. Good show!
   C. You can't spend your life in the restroom, feeling sick. Pretending illness is a cop-out. If you are having trouble at school, ask your teacher or a counselor for help.

By now, you should know a little more about yourself. Are you standing on your own two feet?

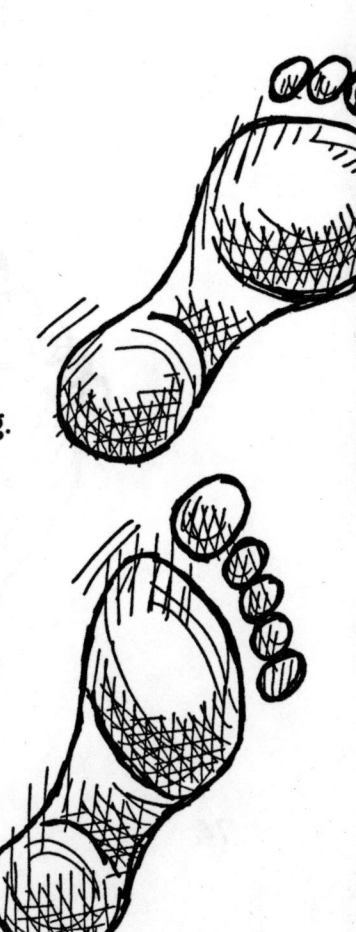

Are you ready to take a giant step forward?

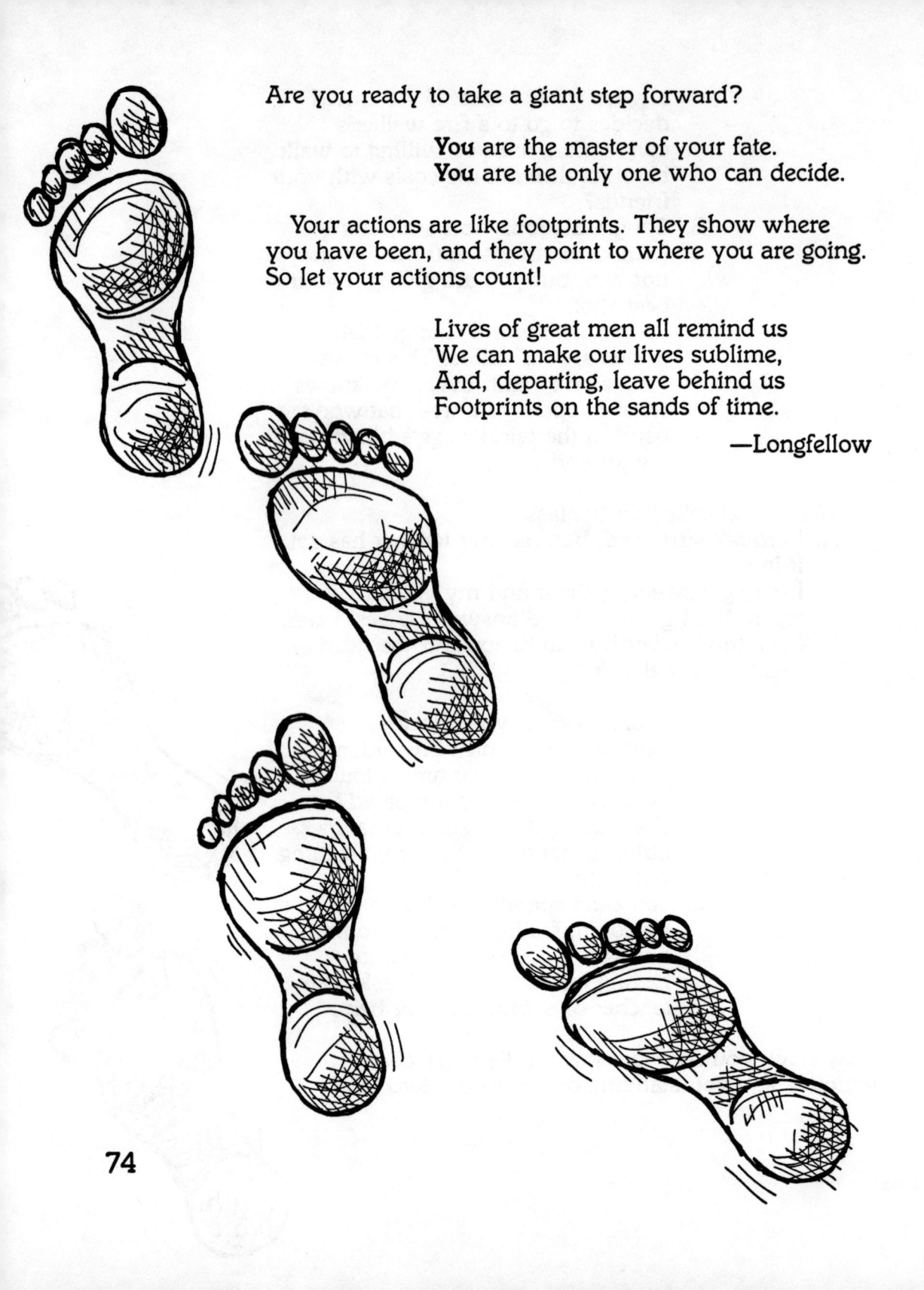

You are the master of your fate.
You are the only one who can decide.

Your actions are like footprints. They show where you have been, and they point to where you are going. So let your actions count!

Lives of great men all remind us
We can make our lives sublime,
And, departing, leave behind us
Footprints on the sands of time.
—Longfellow

CHAPTER NINE
QUESTS, QUESTIONS, AND QUANDARIES

"I'm never sure what I'm going to be, from one minute to another!"

—Lewis Carroll
Alice in Wonderland

During the Middle Ages in lands faraway, it was the custom for all knights to go on **quests**. A quest was a search for something special. It always involved a long journey and a lot of preparation. Knights had to have strong white horses, shiny new armor, feathery plumes for their helmets, and freshly painted shields. Their lances and swords had to be polished and sharpened. According to old storytellers, knights always departed in grand style, with horns blaring and flags waving. Those were important occasions because the knights were setting off to prove their manhood, ready to show the world they were able to pull their own strings.

QUESTS

Quests came in all shapes and sizes. You may have heard of some famous ones such as Jason's quest for the Golden Fleece or King Arthur's quest for the Holy Grail. But the average run-of-the-mill knight was mostly concerned with things like:

> freeing maidens in distress
> fighting fearsome fire-breathing dragons
> solving age-old riddles
> finding the fountain of youth
>   or
> discovering the meaning of life.

Today, there seems to be a shortage of dragons, and nobody wears armor or carries a lance anymore. But that doesn't need to stop you from having a quest of your own, a search for something special, a purpose. You might want to:

> solve the problem of world hunger
> help bring peace to mankind
> eliminate sickness
>   or
> discover new worlds.

Maybe your quest involves a more personal problem, such as:

> passing algebra
> being popular
> getting a job
>   or
> learning to swim.

QUESTIONS

Quests are seldom easy, but they are journeys that are worthwhile. If you haven't found a quest for yourself, perhaps it's time to start asking some questions about:

THE WORLD YOU LIVE IN
YOUR COUNTRY
YOUR TOWN
YOUR FAMILY
YOUR FRIENDS.

You might want to ask:

WHAT: What needs to be done?
WHERE: Where could I start?
WHEN: Is the time right?
WHY: Is it worth doing?
WHO: Who can help me?

QUANDARIES

Sometimes questions lead to quandaries. A quandary is a hard spot to be in. When you are in a quandary, you have a problem without a good answer. It seems that any choice you make will be a bad one. You just don't know what to do. You need help.

When people need help, they often ask for advice. Advice can come from many directions. Some advice is good and some is not so good. The trouble with many advisers is that they like to tell you what **they** think you should do. This is just another example of others pulling your strings.

TALKING TO GOD

God is not a string puller. He is your greatest help even though he never **tells** you what to do.

When you take time to talk to God, he opens your inner eyes so that you can see inside yourself. He helps you work out your own answers. God helps you make choices.

A visit with God is called **prayer**. People pray in many ways. You can pray with your eyes closed. You can pray with your eyes open. You can pray standing up or sitting down—in church or at home or outside in a garden. It doesn't matter how you pray. What matters is that you open your mind to God. How do you do it?

1. **Find a place where you can be quiet and think.** Some people like to be all by themselves. Others can find a quiet place inside themselves—even when they are on a noisy bus.
2. **Talk to God.** You can talk with your inner voice, or you can talk out loud. It doesn't matter to God. Tell him your problems. Tell him how you feel.

God wants you to tell him when you are upset

God wants you to tell him when you are calm

God wants you to tell him when you are sad

God wants you to tell him when you are happy.

You might even want to say:

"I'm sorry"
or
"Thank you."

3. **Be quiet.** Sit still a moment. Sense his peace inside you.
4. **Have confidence.** Know that God has heard you and that he will answer. He always does. Not always in the way that you expect, but always in the way that is best for you.

Praying is a way of putting yourself in God's hands. When you put your life in God's hands, you do not become a puppet. You gain **direction**. You gain **purpose.**

God helps you think for yourself—all through your life.

> Be not simply good—
> Be good for something.
>
> —Thoreau

CHAPTER TEN
STAND UP AND BE COUNTED

Mahomet made the people believe that he would call a hill to him, ... Mahomet called the hill ... again and again; and when the hill stood still, he ... said, "If the hill will not come to Mahomet, Mahomet will go to the hill."

—Francis Bacon

Mahomet was a man who lived many years ago. Of course, he knew that the hill wasn't going to get up and walk. He was just trying to teach this lesson: you don't get things done by waiting around for them to happen. You have to do some things yourself. You have to stand up and be counted.

People who sit around and wait for mountains to move are letting life pass them by. They are **spectators**. This means that they sit on the sidelines, but they don't join the game. They have a strange disease called **spectatoritis**.

People who have **spectatoritis** often have a special problem called **shyness**. This means they are more comfortable with themselves than with other people. They find it hard to join in.

Everyone is shy sometimes. How shy are you? Take the **Timidity Test** and see. Answer the questions as honestly as you can.

TIMIDITY TEST

	YES	NO	SOMETIMES
1. Do you have fun at parties?			
2. Do you look people in the eye when you speak to them?			
3. Do you try to make the new kid in class welcome?			
4. Do you raise your hand in class when you know the answer?			
5. Do you like people to look at you?			
6. Do you blush often and wish you didn't?			
7. Do you think you are awkward or clumsy?			
8. Do you like being by yourself?			
9. When the teacher asks for volunteers, do you feel like hiding?			
10. When you make a mistake, do you worry about it for a long time?			
TOTALS			

Score your test this way:

Questions 1-5:
 Yes—10 points
 No—0 points
 Sometimes—5 points

Questions 6-10:
 Yes—0 points
 No—10 points
 Sometimes—5 points

Now add up ALL your points from all three columns. Your total score is _____.

If you got 60 or more, you don't have a shyness problem. You do pull your own strings. But you might try standing back once in a while to give someone else the spotlight.

If you got between 35 and 55, you seem to be handling yourself onstage OK without trying to steal the limelight from anyone else. You are in control, and you are honest about your feelings. Good for you.

If you got between 0 and 30, you need to work on a new act. Your shyness is keeping you from having a lot of fun. It is giving you **spectatoritis**.

The problem with shyness is that everybody pulls your strings in all directions. Everybody but you.

Sometimes you act the way people want you to, and sometimes you don't do anything at all.

Fourteen-year-old Amy Baker is pretty, smart, creative, and thoughtful. However, nobody knows how nice she is because Amy is so shy.

Every time a boy says, "Hello," Amy's face turns beet red. When one of Amy's teachers calls on her, Amy stands up and shakes all over. At parties, Amy worries about spilling the punch. She never argues. She never asks, "Why?" She always does as she is told, so everybody tells her what to do. Because of her shyness habit, Amy acts like a puppet.

When Amy doesn't stand up for herself, she feels more and more..

>AFRAID
>INSECURE
>HESITANT
>NERVOUS
>and
>ANXIOUS.

If you feel the way Amy does, it's time to make a change. Habits can be broken, and you can break the shyness habit if you try.

BREAKING THE SHYNESS HABIT

1. **Break the ice.** Use your vocal cords. Say, "Hi!" to someone today. It's a one-syllable word requiring no more effort than breathing in and out. You don't have to wait until somebody speaks to you. Go ahead and speak first. Try to remember to smile. (Sometimes it helps to practice before you leave the house.)

2. **Break the news.** Say something nice to another person. You can't go wrong when you give a sincere compliment: "Gee, I love that cute blouse!" or "What a neat watch! Is it new?" or "Congratulations. I heard you made the team." Everybody loves to hear good news.

3. **Break in.** Join the chatter. This doesn't mean that you should be rude. Just wait for a natural pause in the conversation, and then say what you think. You might be surprised to find out that people are interested in your opinion. If you have trouble getting started, try this trick: clear your throat or cough to give yourself an extra second or two to think.

4. **Break up.** When something tickles your funny bone, don't swallow your giggle. Go ahead and laugh. Let it come right out. Laughter is contagious if it is sincere. Before you know it, other people will be laughing, too. Most of all, they will be laughing **with** you, not **at** you.

5. **Break bread.** "Breaking bread" is an ancient phrase that means "eating together." Invite your friends to a party at your house, and "break bread" with them. Being the host or the hostess at a party is one of the best ways in the world to break the shyness habit. When you are helping other people enjoy themselves, you don't have time to be shy.

Overcoming shyness means cutting a lot of strings. It means doing something for yourself. It means standing up and being counted.

That is as good as moving a mountain . . .

any day!

CONCLUSION
PUT YOUR BEST FOOT FORWARD

Long, long ago, so the story goes, there was a puppet made of wood. He was a little different from other puppets because he could walk, talk, and think. His problem was that he was easily influenced. He let all kinds of people pull his strings, and this got him into more trouble than he could handle.

He grew a long nose, got swallowed by a giant fish, and even sprouted donkey ears. His name was Pinocchio. Remember him?

Pinocchio had only one dream—to become a real person. This wasn't going to be easy for him because he never seemed to be able to think for himself. Pinocchio couldn't stand on his own two

feet. He had never learned to pull his own strings.
   After a long time and a lot of adventures, Pinocchio was finally able to understand what being a real person is all about.

He had learned some important things:

> He had learned to work and to stop being lazy.
> He had learned to make up his own mind.
> He had learned to say, "No."
> He had learned how to be sorry.
> He had learned how to be glad.
> He had learned how to "stick with it."
> He had learned how to be kind.
> He had learned the value of true friends.

Because Pinocchio learned his lessons well, he came to know the meaning of:

>FAITHFULNESS
>GENEROSITY
>DILIGENCE
>COURAGE
>HONOR
>TRUTH
> and
>LOVE.

At last, in reward for his kind heart, he was forgiven for his past mischief. Pinocchio became a real person.

Pulling **your** own strings does not mean you can do anything in the world you want to do. As Pinocchio learned, it does not mean freedom without responsibility.
It does mean being a mature, thoughtful, independent human being. It means being a **real** person.